ANTELOPES

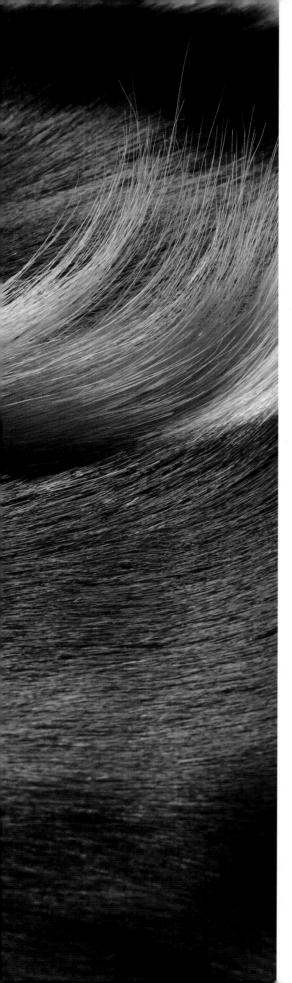

LIVING WILD

Published by Creative Education
P.O. Box 227, Mankato, Minnesota 56002
Creative Education is an imprint of The Creative Company
www.thecreativecompany.us

Design and production by Mary Herrmann
Art direction by Rita Marshall
Printed in the United States of America

Photographs by Alamy (blickwinkel, Corbis Nomad, DBI Studio, Chris Selby), Dreamstime (Mikhail Blajenov, Tiziano Casalta, Enjoyphoto, lorboaz, Alan Lucas, Squareplum, Joel Witmeyer, Xidong Luo), Getty Images (Anup Shah), Shutterstock (Susan Adams, Magdalena Bujak, Jiri Cvrk, Jim David, fotum, Four Oaks, Chris Fourie, Karel Gallas, HPH Image Library, InnaFelker, Gail Johnson, trevor kittelty, Ivan Kuzmin, George Lamson, LFRabanedo, John Lindsay-Smith, Daleen Loest, meunierd, michaeljung, Wendy Nero, Alta Oosthuizen, Stanislav Popov, J Reineke, S1001, Uryadnikov Sergey, Simon_g, SouWest Photography, Villiers Steyn, Johan Swanepoel, Mogens Trolle, Stefanie Van Der Vinden, wcpmedia, worldswildlifewonders, Oleg Znamenskiy)

Library of Congress Cataloging-in-Publication Data
Gish, Melissa.
Antelopes / by Melissa Gish.
p. cm. — (Living wild)
Includes index.
Summary: A look at antelopes, including their habitats, physical characteristics such as their permanent horns, behaviors, relationships with humans, and protected status in the world today.
ISBN 978-1-60818-284-8
1. Antelopes—Juvenile literature. I. Title.

QL737.U53G56 2013
599.64—dc23   2012023242

First Edition
9 8 7 6 5 4 3 2 1

CREATIVE EDUCATION

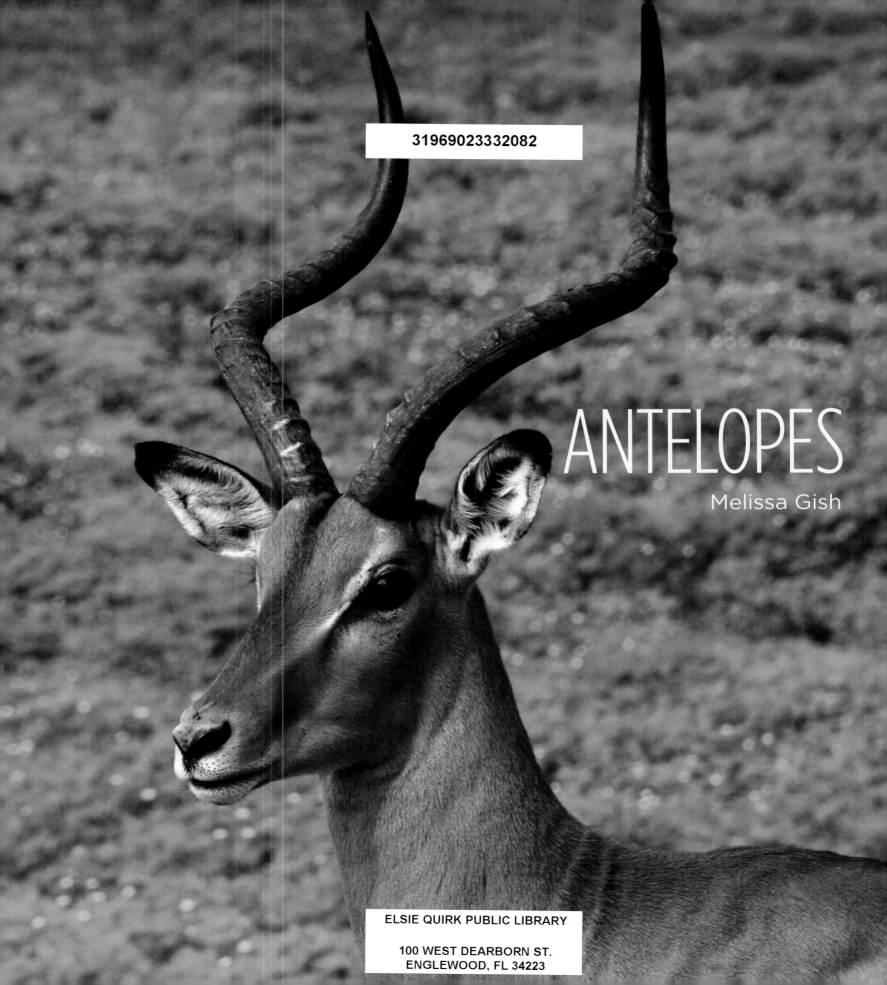

ANTELOPES

Melissa Gish

On a sweltering afternoon in Botswana's
Okavango Delta, a herd of impalas grazes

on lush grass in the shade of an ebony tree.

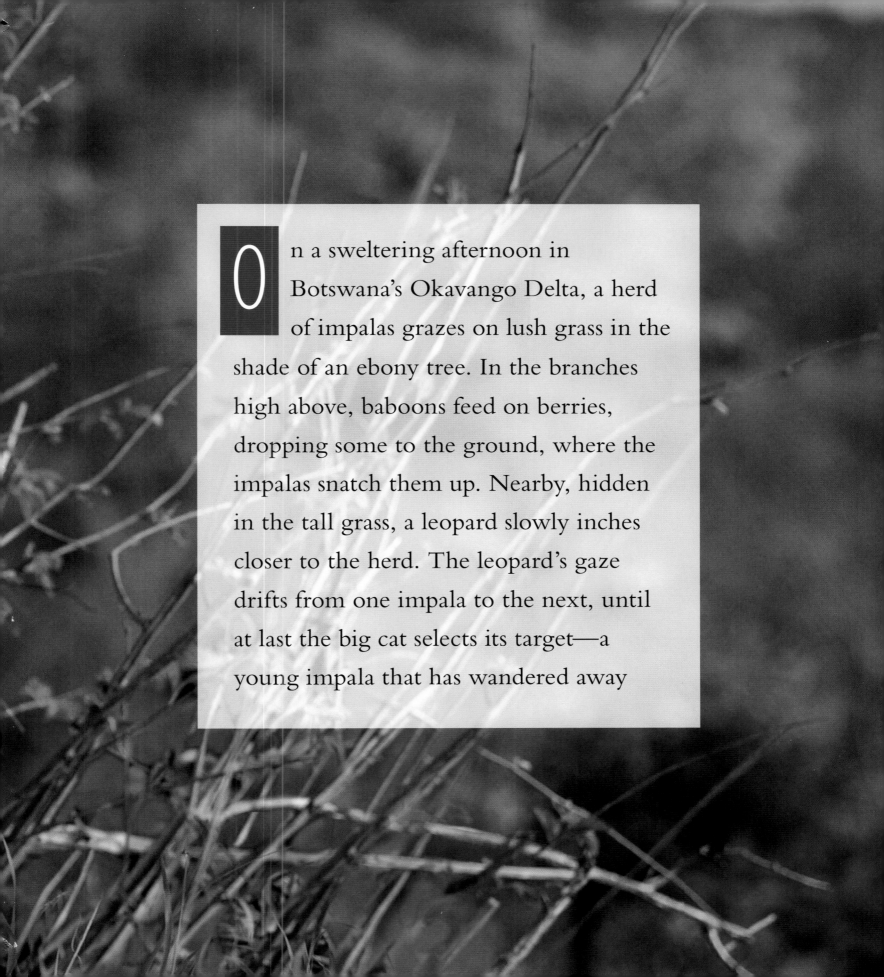

On a sweltering afternoon in Botswana's Okavango Delta, a herd of impalas grazes on lush grass in the shade of an ebony tree. In the branches high above, baboons feed on berries, dropping some to the ground, where the impalas snatch them up. Nearby, hidden in the tall grass, a leopard slowly inches closer to the herd. The leopard's gaze drifts from one impala to the next, until at last the big cat selects its target—a young impala that has wandered away

from its mother. Suddenly, the leopard explodes from the grass toward its prey. The impalas scatter, screeching loudly in alarm. The baboons cry out and shake the tree branches, causing the startled leopard to leap short of its prey. Catching only a glancing blow from the leopard's paw, the young impala escapes—for now. The leopard slinks back into the grass. It will follow the impalas and try for another meal when they regroup.

WHERE IN THE WORLD THEY LIVE

■ **Impala**
southern and
eastern Africa

■ **Thomson's
Gazelle**
Serengeti,
eastern Africa

■ **Springbok**
southwestern
Africa

■ **Gerenuk**
eastern Africa

■ **Black Wildebeest**
central South
Africa

■ **Western
Hartebeest**
western and west-
central Africa

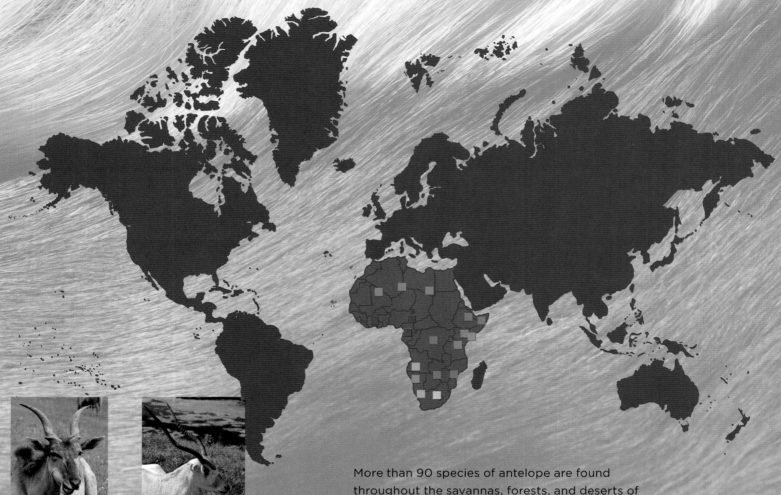

■ **Common Eland**
southern and
eastern Africa

■ **Addax**
Sahara Desert

More than 90 species of antelope are found
throughout the savannas, forests, and deserts of
Africa and in parts of Asia. Some species, such as
impala, have populations numbering in the millions,
while others, such as addax, are critically endangered
in the wild. The eight antelopes shown here represent
a sampling of familiar African species' ranges.

RUNNING FOR THEIR LIVES

The 91 species of antelope are members of the family Bovidae, a group of cloven-hoofed, hollow-horned animals. Other bovids include about 50 antelope relatives such as muskoxen, sheep, goats, and bison. The earliest ancestors of bovids **evolved** about 20 to 18 million years ago in southern Asia and Africa. These small, horned animals, called *Eotragus*, are known from fossilized horn cores found in western Europe and northern Africa.

Over the millennia, prehistoric antelopes spread all across Europe, Africa, and Asia. However, by about 2.5 million years ago, they began disappearing from Europe, which was growing too cold for them. The antelopes in the warmer climates of Africa and Asia flourished. Today, most antelope species inhabit a variety of habitats in Africa, from the lowland forests of the Republic of the Congo and the moist woodlands of Sudan to the subdesert of Namibia, the African nation with the driest climate. Several species, such as the rare saiga antelope, live on the steppes of Central Asia, and a few scarce species, such as the saola, live in Southeast Asian jungles.

The addax can survive temperatures upwards of 130 ˚F (54 ˚C) in the Sahara Desert.

Habitat loss and predation have made Niger's addax the world's rarest antelope species, with fewer than 300 left on Earth.

The royal antelope appeared on this one-cent stamp from the Republic of Liberia in 1942.

The eland is the slowest-running antelope species, but it can jump over a nearly 10-foot-tall (3 m) fence from a standing position.

Antelopes are mammals. All mammals produce milk to feed their young and, with the exceptions of the egg-laying platypuses and hedgehog-like echidnas of Australia, give birth to live offspring. Mammals are also warm-blooded. This means that their bodies try to maintain a healthy, constant temperature that is usually warmer than their surroundings. Antelopes live in hot climates and cool themselves by sweating—just like humans. The sweat **evaporates** to cool the blood just beneath the skin. Antelopes sometimes also pant like dogs, which reduces their internal body temperature.

Adult male antelopes are called bucks, and females are called does. Baby antelopes are called calves. Antelopes vary greatly in size. The world's largest antelope is the giant eland of central Africa. Males of this species, which are slightly bigger than females, can grow to 11 feet (3.4 m) in length and can measure up to 6 feet (1.8 m) tall at the shoulder. They can weigh as much as 2,000 pounds (907 kg). The smallest antelope is the royal antelope, which reaches no more than 10 inches (25.4 cm) tall at the shoulder and weighs no more than 7 pounds (3.2 kg). Royal antelopes live in

Male elands have tufts of hair on their foreheads, which they typically rub in mud and urine during courtship displays.

The male greater kudu's horns can grow to be six feet (1.8 m) long and make two and a half twists.

the undergrowth of forests in northwestern Africa.

Antelope fur is short and stiff, much like that of cows. Some species have a mane of longer hair like a horse's; others have beards that hang from the neck and chin. An antelope's fur color helps it blend in with its surroundings, making it less detectable by predators. The southern lesser kudu, an inhabitant of short, thick forests in Tanzania, is brown with white stripes and white bands on its neck and face. Such markings give the illusion of light shining through trees. The eastern bongo's reddish fur helps it fade into the darkness of its dense forest habitat in eastern Africa. The common eland has only a few white stripes on the front of its honey-brown body, allowing it to hide in the tall, dry grass of its southern and eastern African savanna habitat. Some antelopes, such as the addax, change color with the seasons. The addax is pale beige in the spring and summer, and it turns brown for the fall and winter.

As bovids, antelopes are known for their horns, which are permanently attached to their skulls. Unlike the antlers of deer and moose, which are shed seasonally, antelope horns never fall off unless they are broken off,

Though similar in coloring, the lesser kudu (above) weighs about 240 pounds (109 kg), while the greater kudu can reach 695 pounds (315 kg).

and they continue to grow throughout the animal's life. Both males and females of about two-thirds of all antelope species have horns. The horns are made of bone covered with a layer of keratin—the same substance that is found in human fingernails. There is an air pocket between the bone and keratin, which is why bovids are known as hollow-horned animals.

Unlike deer antlers, a pair of antelope horns is unbranched. Some antelopes, such as the rhebok and the oribi, have horns that are simple spikes. Other antelopes, such as the kudu, have complex spirals that are long, heavy, and dangerous to other animals. The horns of the black wildebeest, also called the gnu, curve downward and forward like the letter *u*, while the southern hartebeest's horns zigzag upward like the letter *s*.

An antelope's two toes are each covered by a hoof. Front hooves are larger than back hooves because it is the forelegs that take the weight of the animal as it runs. The antelope spreads its toes apart when it runs so that the foot does not dig into the ground but rather works like a snowshoe to more evenly distribute the animal's weight. Antelopes' walking gaits vary. The klipspringer walks

on the tip of the hoof, like a ballerina. This allows the klipspringer to maneuver on the steep sides of rocky cliffs without falling. The water-loving sitatunga has elongated hooves that, when the toes are splayed, allow the animal to walk over floating vegetation.

Antelopes have short, grinding back teeth called molars, and special stomachs—with four chambers, or sections—allow them to eat highly fibrous food such as shrubs, grasses, and bamboo, which most other animals find indigestible. In the stomach, food passes through the

The word "klipspringer" means "rock jumper" in the Afrikaans language spoken in Namibia and South Africa.

To feed on tall acacia shrubs, the gerenuk typically stands on its hind legs, balancing itself by propping its front legs on the branches.

first chamber, called the rumen, where bacteria and acids soften it. Then the food is regurgitated, or brought back up to the mouth. This food mass, called a cud, is chewed again. When it is swallowed, the cud passes through all four stomach chambers to be fully digested. Antelopes share this trait of cud chewing with cows, sheep, giraffes, llamas, moose, and many other hoofed mammals classified as ruminants.

An antelope's eyes are set on the sides of its head, which allows the animal to see in any direction with only a slight turn of the head. In addition, each of the antelope's eyes has a horizontal pupil, enabling the antelope to see just as well out of the corners of its eyes as it can see straight ahead. Antelopes are prey animals that are hunted by large predators such as lions, hyenas, tigers, cheetahs, and leopards. As prey animals, antelopes can lie down and sleep deeply for no more than a few minutes at a time. They tend to rest occasionally, standing in place while ruminating, or chewing cud, and remaining ever watchful for predators. Sometimes they sit down and doze, keeping their ears alert to any sound and their eyes half-open. At the slightest hint of danger, antelopes run.

To hide from predators, sitatungas (marshbucks) may lie submerged in swamps with only their faces above water.

The common duiker is 1 of 21 species of duiker, which have a habit of diving into thick brush to escape predators.

HANGIN' WITH THE HERD

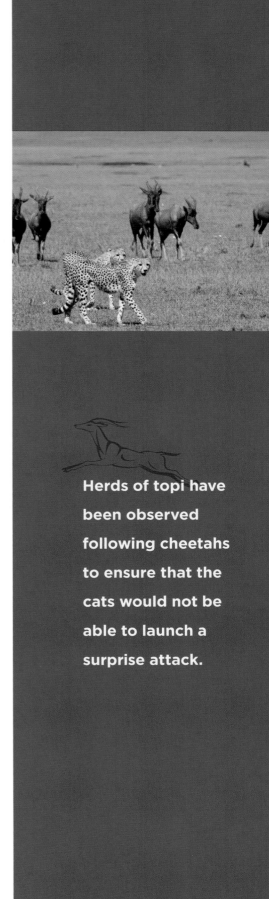

Some antelope species are solitary animals, living alone or in pairs. Like many small forest antelopes, the suni and duikers live alone, defending a small territory from all intruding antelopes. The males and females of these species may share a territory but come together only to mate. Other forest antelopes, including the dik-dik, klipspringer, and oribi, live in breeding pairs or small family herds that work together to defend a territory. Most other antelope species are social, living in groups called bands, harems, or herds, which vary in both size and composition.

Some bands consist of all females and their immature offspring, while others, called bachelor bands, consist of all young males. There is no leadership in bands, and many members come and go, joining different bands throughout the year. Like many antelope species, wildebeest form bands, and during certain times of the year, their bands may merge to form herds consisting of thousands of individuals.

About 90 percent of antelope species are territorial. Mature male antelopes establish territories and form

Herds of topi have been observed following cheetahs to ensure that the cats would not be able to launch a surprise attack.

Male oryx of all ages spar with each other, typically early in the morning, to establish rank in the herd.

The Arabian oryx may have sparked the myth of the unicorn, because an oryx viewed from the side appears to have just one horn.

harems by gathering a group of 2 to 5 does and their offspring—and eventually amassing anywhere from 5 to 65 animals. The buck will mate only with members of his harem, and he will prevent other males from approaching them. Young bucks build their harems by invading existing harems and stealing young females. Bucks mark their territory, which usually ranges from 5 to 40 square miles (13–104 sq km), by urinating and leaving dung as markers around the boundaries. The males of many antelope species have glands on their hind legs just above their hooves that leave scent markers as the animal walks through grass. Harems typically do not enter rival territories, but if they do wander into another buck's domain, they may be met with stomping, charging, or, in some cases, a head-first attack with deadly horns.

For some antelopes, such as the hartebeest, a territory is defended for only part of the year, usually when food is most plentiful and during mating season. Some antelopes, including waterbucks and Grant's gazelles, form large herds of up to 500 members that include males and females of all ages. They live and graze together in one **home range** during the dry winter season and in a

different home range during the rainy summer season.
The animals must move from place to place in order to
feed on certain plants and grasses that are available only
during the winter or the summer seasons.

Some home ranges are not far from each other.
Others are located great distances apart. Some antelope
species, including wildebeest, Thomson's gazelle, and
topi, seasonally **migrate** over thousands of square miles.
Migration is triggered by annual rainfall (which leads to
changes in the food supply that antelopes seek) as well

*Male Grant's gazelles have long,
muscular necks, the strength of
which determines their level of
dominance over other bucks.*

Waterbucks seldom stray far from their water sources, which they share with other wildlife such as Marabou storks.

as the availability of water. Some antelopes, such as the waterbuck and wildebeest, must drink water every day to survive. Other species, including the addax and gerenuk, drink water only when it is readily available, since they can get the moisture they need from their food.

While many succulent plants in antelopes' habitats may appear dry and dead during the arid heat of the day, containing only about 1 percent moisture, these same plants soak up water at night, swelling to contain as much as 30 percent moisture—plenty to sustain many species of antelope that consume the plants. Some antelope species, particularly those that live in forested areas, never drink water, even though it is often nearby. Dik-diks, for example, consume all the moisture they need from the flowers, leaves, and fruit they eat.

Antelope survival depends on the availability of food and the health and strength of the animal. Small antelopes rely on **camouflage**, and unless they exhibit the scent of sickness, they can often hide upwind from predators. A healthy large antelope can usually outrun a predator, but a young, weak, or sick antelope will typically be the first to fall prey to a hungry lion or cheetah in Africa or a tiger or leopard in Asia. Even eagles may drop from the sky to snatch small antelopes that cannot maneuver quickly.

Antelopes of small-sized species, which have shorter life spans, may become sexually mature by six months of age, while larger antelopes must be three or four years old before they can reproduce. Many small antelopes, including dik-diks, duikers, and klipspringers, mate for life. Other antelope species are polygamous, meaning they have more than one mating partner. For most large antelope species, dominant males typically breed with receptive

When most antelope calves are young and helpless, camouflage is their main defense against predators.

Only male lechwe have horns, which they use to challenge each other in a lek, a behavior called lekking.

females in their herd. However, some species, such as the tsessebe (*TAY-seh-bee*) and the lechwe (*LEECH-wee*), exhibit a unique mating habit. Mature males gather in an area called a lek, which serves as a sort of arena in which the bucks fight by shoving each other and crashing their horns together. The winners remain in the lek, while the losers rejoin the herd. The winners are then approached by mature females, who select several partners for mating.

Mating season for antelopes varies by geographic location and climate. Antelopes that live in places affected by seasonal weather changes have one mating season a year. However, most antelopes that live in consistently tropical climates may mate twice a year. The **gestation** period of antelopes varies from four to nine months, with smaller species giving birth sooner than larger species. Woodland antelope species give birth to one or two calves in a spot hidden from predators, where the calves will remain for several weeks. The calves' only defense is their camouflaged fur. Antelopes that live on the open savanna are born ready to move. Within 15 minutes of birth, a baby wildebeest can run with its herd. The entire herd works together to protect calves from predators.

Antelope calves begin eating grass within the first two or three weeks of life, though they continue to feed on the milk their mothers produce for three or four months. Young antelopes typically stay near their mothers until the next calf is born, at which time the mother drives away the older offspring. Depending on the species, a yearling may wander away to find a mate, join a bachelor band, or stay in its family herd. Whichever life it chooses, if it can avoid predation, a healthy antelope may live as long as 15 to 25 years.

Hartebeest feed on their mother's milk for four months and reach their full adult size after four years.

In Dogon tradition, masks are carved and decorated in private, away from the village, and displayed only once complete.

ANTELOPE DANCING

The speed and grace of antelopes have led many African **cultures** to view antelopes as symbols of power and mystery. To the Bambara people of the Republic of Mali, the antelope is the traditional symbol of farming, which is vital to the Bambaras' way of life. Chi Wara, the Bambara god of agriculture, is represented as both male and female, with the head of a human and the body of a roan antelope. The Bambara carve elaborate wooden figures of the female Chi Wara, which has straight horns and is paired with a baby antelope, and male Chi Wara, which has curved horns. Wearing carved, painted, wooden Chi Wara masks, the Bambara perform the Chi Wara dance as a celebration of the time in their ancient history when the antelope god taught humans how to farm the land.

The remaining 300,000 Dogon people who inhabit hundreds of tiny villages along Mali's Bandiagara Cliffs retain strong traditional beliefs in the power of antelopes. Most Dogon practice an **animist** religion in which the antelope is believed to restore strength to a village after a village member's death. The antelope's restorative power

Male roan antelope have darker face masks, heavier bodies, and longer horns than females.

In 1992, a nature reserve was established around the Voortrekker Monument, and in 2011, it was declared a National Heritage Site.

is celebrated in music and dance, with elaborately carved wooden antelope masks, called *karandas*, worn by the Dogon during their ritual *dama* dances.

On the Asian continent, the Kurumba people of southern India hold to their traditional beliefs in the antelope's power. Large antelope headdresses feature long necks and long snouts. Some versions include a face-covering mask. The headdresses are painted with geometric patterns using natural substances such as mud and charcoal for black, ocher clay for red, and kaolinite clay for white. The roan antelope is the **totem** animal of most Kurumba tribes, so this is the type of antelope represented by most headdresses. The Kurumba use the headdresses to commemorate three major periods in the tribe's cycle of death. First, the headdresses are worn during a burial. The antelopes symbolize the spirits of the deceased person's ancestors presiding over the burial. Several weeks later, the headdresses are worn during a ceremony to honor the deceased and free his or her spirit to join the ancestors in the afterlife. Some months after that, the headdresses are worn again as the Kurumba make sacrifices to the ancestors and ask the antelope spirit to protect them in the coming year.

Wildebeest are featured on the Voortrekker Monument, which towers over the landscape near Pretoria, South Africa. The monument honors the Voortrekkers—pioneers who traveled from what is now Cape Town to settle a number of wilderness areas in South Africa between 1835 and 1854. The monument includes a domed ceiling as well as carved images and statues on its interior and exterior stone walls. At the foot of the monument stands a bronze statue of a woman with two children, representing the family spirit of the pioneers, flanked by black wildebeest carved into the walls as symbols of the dangers faced by those who ventured into the untamed land.

Wildebeest must drink every other day, so they try to avoid traveling more than 15 miles (24.1 km) from a water source.

Bushman cave art was created by applying thick paint (made from crushed plants and rocks) to the spongelike surface of sandstone.

At more than 11,000 feet (3,353 m), the Drakensberg Mountains are the highest range in southern Africa. These mountains contain many caves and overhangs that are home to the largest collection of Bushman art in the world. (Bushmen are the **indigenous** people of southern Africa.) As many as 40,000 paintings of people and animals—including gazelles, impalas, elands, and other antelope species—have been discovered in 500 different locations. Researchers estimate the age of some of the paintings as being 2,400 years old, but anthropologists (scientists who study the history of humankind) suggest that, since the Bushman culture emerged in the area far earlier, the oldest paintings could date back 40,000 years. Similar prehistoric art has been discovered in the Cederberg Mountains north of Cape Town and in a remote area of the Northern Cape, South Africa, at a site called the Wildebeest Kuil Rock Art Centre.

In addition to the visual stories presented through rock art, the recounting of folk tales is a way people keep their traditions and customs alive. A traditional folk tale from West Java, a province of Indonesia, tells of an old man who happened upon a beautiful golden antelope in the forest. He befriended the antelope, who later cared for him when he fell ill. One day, a prince shot the golden antelope with an arrow. Instead of dying, the antelope turned into a princess. She explained that a witch had cursed her, and she could return to her true form only if she was shot by a prince's arrow. Then the prince asked the princess to marry him, but because the princess still had the tender and kind heart of the golden antelope, she agreed to marry the prince only if she were allowed to take the old man to live at the palace with her—which she did.

Few modern stories feature antelopes as major characters endowed with individual personalities; instead,

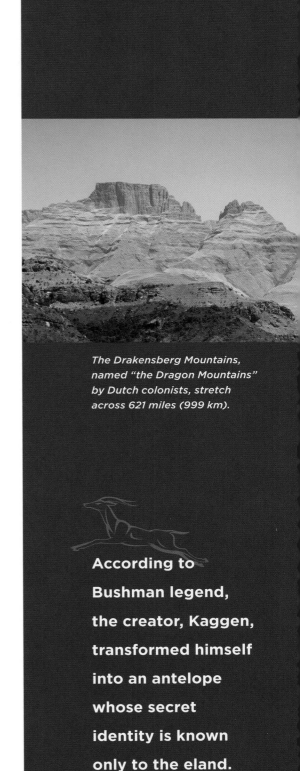

The Drakensberg Mountains, named "the Dragon Mountains" by Dutch colonists, stretch across 621 miles (999 km).

According to Bushman legend, the creator, Kaggen, transformed himself into an antelope whose secret identity is known only to the eland.

THE GAZELLE

Gazella Dorcas

Enchanted thing: how can two chosen words
ever attain the harmony of pure rhyme
that pulses through you as your body stirs?
Out of your forehead branch and lyre climb,

and all your features pass in simile, through
the songs of love whose words, as light as rose-
petals, rest on the face of someone who
has put his book away and shut his eyes:

to see you: tensed, as if each leg were a gun
loaded with leaps, but not fired while your neck
holds your head still, listening: as when,

while swimming in some isolated place,
a girl hears leaves rustle, and turns to look:
the forest pool reflected in her face.

Ranier Maria Rilke (1875–1926)
From New Poems

herds of gazelles, impalas, and wildebeest, in particular, are often presented as elements of the landscape. Antelope herds in animated movies such as *The Lion King* (1994) and *Madagascar: Escape 2 Africa* (2008) represent the vast wilderness of Africa's plains. But real antelopes were the subjects of the 2004 movie *Kekexili: Mountain Patrol*, which was filmed in China. Based on the real-life experiences of people working to save endangered Tibetan antelopes from **poachers**, the movie led to public pressure to enact laws that would provide more protection for the antelopes. Today, about 75,000 Tibetan antelopes remain in the wild.

The antelope's reputation as a graceful and strong animal has extended to many areas of popular culture—even cars. The Chevrolet Impala, introduced in 1958 as the American company's highest-priced luxury automobile, was named after an animal known for its strength and speed. The Chevy Impala holds the record for the highest-selling model of car in a single year—nearly 1.1 million Impalas were sold in 1964. The original rear-wheel-drive Impala is the best-selling car in United States history, with nearly 13 million Impalas sold from 1958 to 1996.

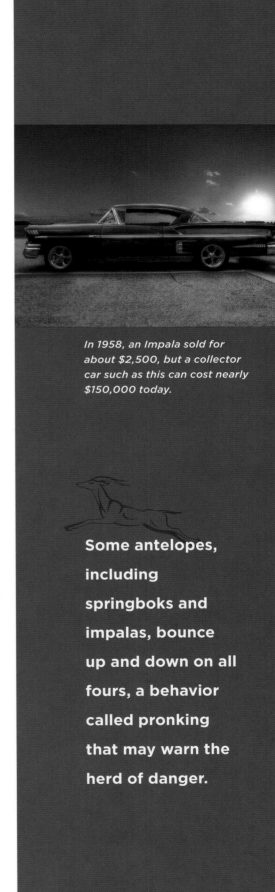

In 1958, an Impala sold for about $2,500, but a collector car such as this can cost nearly $150,000 today.

Some antelopes, including springboks and impalas, bounce up and down on all fours, a behavior called pronking that may warn the herd of danger.

In spring and summer, female Tibetan antelopes migrate to give birth near lakes in the Hoh Xil National Nature Reserve.

MASTERS OF MIGRATION

Egyptian art commonly depicts the giant sable antelope and the falcon as wild animals captured and kept in private collections.

Antelopes have roamed the African continent for thousands of years. Most early species, such as *Megalotragus priscus*, with its long, downward-curving horns, were about 20 percent larger than the largest modern antelopes. *Hippotragus gigas*, an ancestor of the roan antelope, had horns bigger than any modern antelope except for the critically endangered giant sable antelope of Angola. *Hippotragus gigas* thrived in South Africa until about 10,000 years ago.

Despite having many similarities to cattle, antelopes have never been **domesticated** as cattle, oxen, or horses have. Antelopes were captured for royal **menageries** in ancient Egypt, as evidenced by paintings on tomb walls dating from about 2400 B.C. that show gazelles, ibex, and oryx wearing collars and feeding from troughs. Although such indications of attempted domestication exist, no antelope species was ever successfully domesticated on a large scale.

In 1591, the Italian explorer Filippo Pigafetta traveled to what is now Angola and described in his journal the eland, an antelope he believed could "be taught to draw the plough." This idea was not taken seriously for centuries,

Despite being called pronghorn antelope, the North American pronghorn is not a true antelope and is, in fact, unique among all hoofed mammals.

though. It was not until 1842 that two male and one female eland became the first of their kind to be brought to Europe. The 13th Earl of Derby added the elands to his private menagerie in what is now Merseyside, England, where the elands produced two calves. When the Earl attempted to cross the elands with domestic cattle, however, the first results were unwelcome. Records describe the offspring as "ravenous feeders" that required too much food. The breeding program was abandoned almost immediately.

The Earl of Breadalbane introduced the eland into Scotland in 1856. A committee of men from the British Museum of Natural History convened in 1859 to eat one of the elands, which had been sent to London as a gift from Breadalbane. Everyone on the committee agreed that eland was the best meat any of them had ever tasted. Elands were soon dispersed all around the world for experiments in **animal husbandry**; despite the quality of eland meat and milk, however, eland ranching never caught on outside the eland's native Africa. Only in Russia, on a private estate that has since become the Askaniya Nova Zoo, did a herd succeed. From a pair of elands that arrived in 1892, 500 descendants have been born. The herd is fully domesticated today—and the does are regularly milked. Today in Africa, herds of elands and oryx are held in captivity for meat and milk production. Elands require as much food and water as cattle, but oryx thrive on very little grass and only a quarter the amount of water that cattle require, making them desirable livestock in drought-plagued areas of Africa.

Because of its ability to survive on limited resources, the oryx was introduced as a game animal in the dry desert wilderness of White Sands Missile Range in the Tularosa Basin of New Mexico. Laws prohibit the release of foreign wild animals into any U.S. habitat, so only the offspring of the oryx brought from Africa could be released. Between 1969 and 1977, 93 oryx were set loose. Within a few decades, the oryx population began to soar. Each year, the state of New Mexico issues up to 600 once-in-a-lifetime hunting permits to people wishing to hunt oryx on the White Sands Missile Range. The oryx have become so successful that they have outgrown the protected area and have moved into the surrounding mountains and valleys, where they can be hunted by annual permit.

In their native Africa, antelopes are the subjects of much research during the great migrations, when bands

About 600,000 people visit White Sands National Monument annually, but few see the elusive oryx that live there.

Elands form small bands to browse for food but come together in large herds to feed on lush greenery that flourishes after rain.

of wildebeest and Thomson's gazelles join together with other animals to follow the annual rainfall toward greener feeding grounds. The largest antelope migration occurs on the Serengeti Plain of Tanzania and Kenya. Botswana, in southern Africa, is the location of the Makgadikgadi antelope migration, the second-largest migration. This annual event attracted attention in recent years, thanks to coverage such as National Geographic's 2010 television documentary series *Great Migrations*.

Research on antelopes in their native environments provides conservationists with information helpful to the preservation of antelope species. British scientists James Bradley and Chris Brooks of the University of Bristol study the migration of Africa's large mammals, including antelopes. Their research is focused on the impact that thousands of miles of fencing across Botswana and Namibia has on migrating herds, since it blocks the animals from water sources. Nearby, researchers with the World Association of Zoos and Aquariums (WAZA) study Zimbabwe's eight antelope species, five of which appear on the Red List of Threatened Species that is published annually by the International Union for Conservation of

Nature (IUCN). Studies conducted in the wild gather information on how antelopes help shape their **ecosystems**, and **captive-bred** antelopes of seven Zimbabwean species are kept in naturalistic enclosures in Zimbabwe's Dambari Field Station in an effort to maintain healthy breeding populations of these antelopes. The WAZA researchers hope to formulate long-term strategies for conservation of the antelope species most at risk of extinction.

The IUCN's Antelope Specialist Group conducts research on antelopes around the world in efforts to bring back dwindling antelope populations and restore lost or damaged habitats that antelopes need in order to survive. The

About one quarter of migrating wildebeest die during their annual journey, but twice as many more are born each year.

Running in circles and pronking are ways that springboks spread territory-marking scent from their foot glands.

Convention on Migratory Species is another organization that has been working to restore antelope populations. One of its major projects has been the captive-breeding and reintroduction of addax and oryx into the native Tunisian habitats from which they were nearly wiped out by environmental destruction and poaching. The first animals were released in 2007. Twenty addax were taken to the Saharan Jebil National Park and Senghar National Park, and 10 scimitar-horned oryx, which were previously considered extinct in the wild, were taken to Dghoumes National Park. To expand **genetic** diversity among the species, nearly two dozen addax and oryx were collected from zoos around the world and released into the parks as well.

Although there are many kinds of antelope, more than a quarter of all species are at risk of extinction. Only one species, the South African springbok, has responded to recent conservation efforts and shown an increase in population. Overhunting for food, poaching, habitat destruction, and drought have devastated many other populations. Conservation measures are needed to bring many antelope species back from the brink and protect the great herds that still roam their natural environments.

Reedbucks may emit a high-pitched whistle through their nostrils to warn of danger before attempting to escape.

Frightened reedbucks lie flat on the ground with their necks outstretched, then jump up and run away at the last moment.

ANIMAL TALE: HOW TSESSEBE GOT HIS HORNS

The indigenous peoples of Africa have long valued antelopes as a source of food and clothing, and antelopes were often the main characters in adventure stories and traditional pourquoi, which are stories that explain how things came to be. The following pourquoi from the Bushman tradition of South Africa tells how the common tsessebe got its horns.

Long ago, the Creator spent many days and nights making all the animals. When he finished, he was very tired and lay down for a long nap, not realizing that he had forgotten to give Tsessebe any horns. At the watering hole, Gerenuk with his spiraling horns, Wildebeest with his U-shaped horns, Lechwe with his long, sweeping horns, and all the other antelopes with horns in many different shapes and sizes laughed at Tsessebe, whose head was bare.

Tsessebe felt sad. He wandered the savanna for a long time, wondering why the Creator had forgotten about him. He even stopped going to the watering hole to avoid being laughed at by the other antelopes. Tired and thirsty, Tsessebe finally decided to approach the Creator and ask for some horns.

The Creator, exhausted from his work, was still sleeping when Tsessebe went to him. "What do you want?" the Creator snapped at Tsessebe. "Can't you see I am resting?"

"I am very sorry," said Tsessebe, "but I must ask why you forgot to give me horns like the other antelopes."

Further annoyed at being accused of forgetfulness, the Creator mimicked Tsessebe's voice. "Forgot to give you horns?" He picked up Tsessebe and turned him from

side to side. "Who says I forgot? Maybe I chose to leave you bareheaded."

"Oh my," said Tsessebe, "I did not mean to suggest you made a mistake. But I would like it very much if you would choose to give me some horns."

Still sleepy and crabby, the Creator picked up two old bones from beside his campfire. He stuck the bones on top of Tsessebe's head, and then he dropped Tsessebe to the ground. "There," the Creator grumbled. "You have horns. Now go away and leave me alone."

Tsessebe reached up and felt his horns, which were only slightly bent and rather plain. He hung his head in sadness. *Well*, he thought, *at least these horns are better than no horns at all*. And he began to walk away.

The Creator loved all his creations, even the ones that annoyed him—like Tsessebe. "Wait," said the Creator. "You were brave to come here and ask for horns. Let me give you a gift."

Tsessebe stopped and turned to face the Creator. "A gift?" he said. "But you gave me horns as I asked."

"Those horns are ugly," admitted the Creator. "Let me give you something no one else has." Then the Creator touched Tsessebe's front hooves, endowing Tsessebe with a speed and agility that no other antelope species possessed.

When Tsessebe returned to the watering hole, the other antelopes laughed at his horns. But then Tsessebe ran. He ran in wide circles, laughing at the other antelopes. He no longer cared about his horns because he could now run faster than any other antelope, and the other antelopes envied this talent. Because of the Creator's gift, the common tsessebe is not only the fastest antelope species but also the fastest hoofed mammal in the world.

GLOSSARY

animal husbandry – the science and practice of breeding and caring for farm animals

animist – related to a religious belief in which plants, animals, and other natural phenomena have spiritual relevance and power

camouflage – the ability to hide, due to coloring or markings that blend in with a given environment

captive-bred – bred and raised in a place from which escape is not possible

cultures – particular groups in a society that share behaviors and characteristics that are accepted as normal by that group

domesticated – tamed to be kept as a pet or used as a work animal

ecosystems – communities of organisms that live together in environments

evaporates – changes from liquid to invisible vapor, or gas

evolved – gradually developed into a new form

genetic – relating to genes, the basic physical units of heredity

gestation – the period of time it takes a baby to develop inside its mother's womb

home range – an area over which an animal or group of animals regularly travels while searching for food or mates

indigenous – originating in a particular region or country

menageries – collections of wild or unique animals that are kept on display

migrate – undertake a regular, seasonal journey from one place to another and then back again

poachers – people who hunt protected species of wild animals, even though doing so is against the law

totem – an object, animal, or plant respected as a symbol of a tribe and often used in ceremonies or rituals

SELECTED BIBLIOGRAPHY

African Wildlife Foundation. "Wildlife: Eland." http://www.awf.org/content/wildlife/detail/eland.

Gilman International Conservation Foundation. "Animal Programs: Eastern Bongo." White Oak Conservation Center. http://www.wocenter.org/bongo-eastern.asp.

Mungall, Elizabeth Cary. *Exotic Animal Field Guide: Nonnative Hoofed Animals in the United States*. College Station: Texas A&M University Press, 2007.

San Diego Zoo. "Animal Bytes: Antelope." http://www.sandiegozoo.org/animalbytes/t-antelope.htm.

Shorrocks, Bryan. *The Biology of African Savannahs*. Oxford: Oxford University Press, 2007.

Stuart, Chris, and Tilde Stuart. *Field Guide to the Larger Mammals of Africa*. Cape Town: Struik Nature, 2007.

Oxpeckers are birds that provide antelopes with a cleaning service by eating insects and tiny organisms off the animals' hides.

INDEX